Find Your Voice Abroad

From Self-Doubt to Confident Leadership for International Women

Ina Saltanava

Advance Praise

"I read this and I felt seen. As an ex-CPO of a large multinational company who has built a career across borders, I thought I had figured most of this out. But Ina Saltanava's book hit a nerve I didn't know was still exposed.

This isn't just another fluffy leadership book. It deeply touches every one of us who has felt invisible or undervalued while working abroad, especially women. I've seen the systems from the inside — I know they were 'designed by men for men' — and I know the exhaustion of trying to 'stretch to fit in' just to survive in them. This book calls that out perfectly and call for a discovery of an authentic self aligned with being a female leader.

What I love is that it doesn't tell you to just work harder. It tells you to stop apologizing. The concept of the 'unapologetic edge' resonates so deeply with me. We have these 'leadership superpowers' — adaptability, resilience, cultural intelligence — but we bury them because we are afraid. This book pushes you to find your own true voice that gives you power in spite of that fear.

The A.B.R.O.A.D. framework is actually practical, not just theory. It's about moving from self-doubt to self-trust.

If you are an international woman who is tired of shrinking yourself to fit a mold that wasn't made for you: read this. Claim your space. It is empowering as hell."

— Olga Gebhardt, Executive Partner at Gartner

"Find Your Voice Abroad: From Self-Doubt to Confident Leadership for International Women by Ina Saltanava is a groundbreaking guide for international women navigating the challenges of leadership in foreign environments. Drawing on two decades of personal experience and citing research from leading sources like McKinsey & Company and Grant Thornton, Saltanava highlights the systemic barriers, cultural biases, and gender discrimination that often undermine women's leadership potential abroad. Her A.B.R.O.A.D.™ framework provides a practical and empowering roadmap, helping women recognize their unique strengths – such as adaptability, resilience, and cultural intelligence – and

transform them into leadership superpowers. With a focus on self-awareness, intentional action, and authentic growth, this book inspires women to reclaim their confidence, redefine their future, and lead with impact.

This book is essential reading for women aspiring to thrive in international leadership roles and for organizations striving to foster diversity and inclusion. Saltanava's insights offer strategies that align with transformational and adaptive leadership theories while addressing the urgent need for equity-focused systems. Her framework is not only actionable but also a reliable tool for driving meaningful change. Find Your Voice Abroad is more than a guide – it is a call to action to empower women leaders and reshape global workplaces into inclusive environments where diverse leadership can flourish."

— Dr. Tim Jansa, Higher Education Consultant & ICF and Board-Certified Coach

"Changing women's mindsets to help them reach their full potential — without guilt or feelings of inadequacy — resonates deeply with the shared challenges many female expatriates experience. Written with the heart, this book brings women's leadership to a whole new level. From the very first pages, the author offers valuable insights to women choosing to work abroad on how to overcome professional and personal obstacles. I highly recommend this book to women beginning their professional journeys abroad, as well as to those who feel stuck in their roles and are looking for encouragement to continue growing and advancing in their careers."

— Panagiota Liakopoulou, expatriate
professional at an international
organisation

"Within the first chapters of Ina's book I was surprised to see my own deeply held beliefs reflected back to me by a connection I've only met through the power of LinkedIn which reconfirms that it's not our location which determines our tribe but our energy and intentions to live a brave and true life. Ina writes "Imagine yourself as a painter, and your life as a canvas. First, paint your present self — all the elements that make you who you are today." She goes on to encourage readers to intentionally cultivate their habits, strengths and patterns through thoughtful questions and stories. This book is a roadmap for anyone who wants to build the life of their dreams abroad."

— Samantha Marion, Director of Global
Partnerships; Asian Institute of
Hospitality & Management

"I want to start by saying that this book touched me deeply. Reading it made me feel seen. In many ways, it reassured me that I am not the only one who has experienced lack of recognition and unfair treatment at work.

This book captures these invisible struggles so accurately. As international women, we are sometimes perceived as if we are running away from something, when in reality we are simply curious, ambitious, and free-spirited. It may sound naïve, but it is not.

I truly believe this book will resonate with many women who feel alone in their experiences. The invitation to reflect throughout the chapters is a very smart and powerful choice. At the end of the day, many of us are asking ourselves the same questions, yet we invalidate our own feelings because we are too busy trying to prove our worth in the workplace.

One sentence that deeply impacted me was:

'Say it out loud: Adaptability, resilience, and cultural intelligence are my leadership superpowers.'

Wow! I had never framed it that way before. We need to stop seeing being a foreigner or being a woman as a disadvantage in the workforce, and instead recognize it as a powerful strength.

I also strongly connected with the section about timing. That is exactly what I am navigating right now. Balancing home responsibilities, friends, my partner and his children, medical appointments to manage my health, and still trying to find time to study and pursue a Master's degree in Psychology. In a few years, I will be 42, and I will be 42 whether or not I have that diploma. That perspective really stayed with me.

Throughout the book, I can feel that the author is also doing her own inner work and growing step by step. Each chapter feels focused and intentional. The real-life examples are especially powerful, they allow the reader to see themselves in these women's stories. It feels close, honest, and authentic. That is definitely a strong selling point.

Overall, I believe this book has the potential to reach many hearts and inspire meaningful change."

— Alejandra Lopez Martin, Learning &
Development Expert

This book is a confession from the bottom of my heart. It is a scream into the void. A scream for every woman living abroad who has been silent, invisible, or afraid.

I hope this book becomes a guide for international women who have lived in the shadows for too long, for women who are done hiding — and ready to live the life they truly deserve.

I dedicate this book to every woman who has had the courage to live and work abroad.

To every woman whose voice is still forming, still finding its strength.

And to every man who stands — or will stand — next to women through this change; who has the courage and wisdom to listen, to support, and to recognize that the current system does not serve women and must change.

Contents

Foreword by Jessica D. Winder

There are books that inform. There are books that inspire. And then there are books that quietly name an experience you have lived but never fully had language for. This is that kind of book.

When Ina asked me to write the foreword for *Find Your Voice Abroad*, I said yes immediately. Not because it felt flattering, but because it felt necessary. This is a book that needed to exist, and, more importantly, it needed to be framed by someone who understands both the personal cost and the structural realities of women navigating power, work, and identity within systems that were never designed with them in mind.

I was raised in a small town in Northeast Texas. The kind of place where expectations are set early, the world feels far away, and very few people look like you if you decide to dream bigger. From there, I moved halfway across the world to Sydney, Australia, where I lived for two years while earning my master's degree and working full-time.

I did that as an African American woman.

Living abroad was transformative. It was also isolating, exhausting, and humbling in ways I was not prepared for. I was navigating a new country, new academic expectations, a demanding work environment, and constant visibility all at once. I was different in every room. My accent stood out. My race stood out. My background stood out. There was no blending in.

That experience gave me an early and lasting understanding of what this book so clearly names. When you live and work abroad, you are often asked to adapt without support. To prove yourself repeatedly. To translate who you are in spaces that were not built with you in mind.

Ina didn't choose me because our paths were identical. She chose me because I understand the invisible tax women pay to be perceived as capable. I understand how confidence gets misread, how competence gets questioned, and how silence becomes a survival strategy.

Since that time, I have spent my career at the intersection of people, power, leadership, and systems. I have held executive roles. I have coached leaders across industries. I have watched who gets promoted, who gets protected, and who quietly does the emotional labor that keeps organizations functioning.

I have also worked with countless women who were living or working abroad and slowly losing themselves in the process. Women who were multilingual, globally experienced, emotionally intelligent, and deeply capable, yet still made to feel lucky just to have a seat at the table.

Many of them questioned themselves when the real issue was never them.

The problem was always the system.

This book matters because it tells the truth about that reality without blaming women for the conditions they are navigating.

What stood out to me immediately in Ina's work is that she does not try to fix women.

She does not tell women to lean in harder, soften their edges, or perform confidence until someone else validates it.

Instead, she reframes the entire conversation.

She shows women that adaptability is leadership.

That resilience is earned, not accidental.

That cultural intelligence is not a nice-to-have, but a real competitive advantage.

This book names the loneliness of living abroad. The way confidence erodes when effort is normalized and recognition is withheld. The quiet pressure to be grateful, flexible, and agreeable at all costs.

And then it does something generous.

It offers a path back to self-trust.

If you are an international woman living or working abroad, this book will feel familiar in a way that may be uncomfortable at first. You will recognize moments you thought were isolated. You will see patterns you may have internalized as personal shortcomings.

You will gain language for experiences you may have minimized.

You will gain permission to stop shrinking.

You will gain practical tools to reconnect with your value, your voice, and your direction.

This is not about becoming louder or tougher. It is about becoming more aligned, more intentional, and more grounded in who you are.

By the time you reach the end, you will not just feel seen. You will feel equipped.

Ina writes from lived experience, not theory. She has worked across countries, cultures, and leadership roles. She understands how power operates differently depending on who holds it and who is expected to accommodate it.

What makes her voice credible is not perfection, but integrity. She does not pretend this journey is easy. She does not minimize the compromises women are often pressured to make. And she does not offer quick fixes.

She offers clarity.

She offers structure.

She offers a framework built from walking this path herself and then guiding other women through it with honesty and care.

This book is the result of years of listening to women who felt invisible and helping them reclaim their voice without losing themselves in the process.

This book is not here to impress you.

It is here to meet you where you are.

If you have ever questioned your worth in a room you worked hard to enter, this book is for you.

If you have ever felt invisible while doing everything right, this book is for you.

If you are ready to stop endlessly adapting and start choosing yourself intentionally, this book is for you.

Read it slowly.

Reflect honestly.

Let it challenge you where it needs to.

Finding your voice is not about becoming someone new.

It is about remembering who you already are.

And this book will help you do exactly that.

— Jessica D. Winder, Founder of Hidden Gem Career Coaching, Author of *The Hidden Gem Within*

Foreword by Carolina M. Mata

There are books that inform, and there are books that liberate. What you hold in your hands is the latter.

I met Ina Saltanava the way the best relationships often begin, in the middle of hard work. We were partnered during our coaching certification journey, practicing what we were learning in real time on each other. That's an intimate thing, to be someone's laboratory and to let them be yours. What emerged wasn't just a professional rapport; it was a genuine connection built on mutual trust, honesty, and a shared belief that growth requires courage.

Ina asked me to write this foreword, and I said yes without hesitation. Not because it was easy, but because I knew I had something true to say.

I'll be honest: vulnerability doesn't come naturally to me. I've built my career, and in many ways, my identity, on being the person who figures it out, who keeps going, who delivers. As a single mother climbing toward senior leadership at some of the world's largest organizations, I learned early that self-reliance was my armor. What I didn't always recognize was how much that armor weighed.

Ina made space for me to put it down.

In our work together, she created the conditions for me to be weak so that I could become stronger. To give myself grace. To find my next step forward rather than simply pushing through. I am eternally grateful for that, and it is precisely why I trust her — and this book — completely.

I haven't lived the expat experience that anchors Ina's framework. I am a Hispanic woman who built her career in Fortune 100 companies, navigating the particular challenge of needing to belong while also standing apart. Of balancing the risk of speaking up against the cost of staying silent. Of owning ambition while protecting income. Of wanting to lead authentically while quietly wondering whether the space at the table was really mine.

Sound familiar?

That's what struck me most about the A.B.R.O.A.D.™ framework. Yes, Ina designed it for international women navigating foreign workplaces. But its power extends far beyond geography. Whether you've crossed an ocean or simply walked into a room where you weren't sure you belonged, this framework meets you there. It is an executable, sustainable platform for continuous reflection and growth, and for anyone motivated to become more fully themselves, that is a compelling promise.

The book you are about to read is both deeply personal and rigorously practical. Ina doesn't theorize from a distance. She lived these challenges — working across six countries, reporting exclusively to men, overdelivering while being underestimated, carrying invisible weight with a visible smile. She transformed her own experience into a framework that transforms others. I have watched her do it.

I have also watched Ina do something harder: invest in herself. When we first met, she was pouring everything into her job, her family, her mission, and leaving little for herself. Over time, I watched her consciously make space, use her voice, and stand up — for others and for herself. That is what this book asks of you. And she will not ask you to do anything she hasn't done first.

In these pages, you will find tools to name your strengths when the world has convinced you they don't count. You will find permission to redefine yourself on your own terms. You will find a path from self-doubt to grounded confidence, not the performed kind, but the kind that holds.

Turn the page. Ina is waiting for you…and so

is the version of yourself you've been putting off becoming.

— Carolina M. Mata ACC, BCC;
Senior Vice President, Employee
Communications at Integral;
Board Director, Culture and Belonging at
ICF Connecticut Charter Chapter;
Named 2026 Top Women in
Communication, Ragan

Chapter 1

The System That Silences You

*"When I dare to be powerful, to use my
strength in the service of my vision, then it
becomes less and less important whether I
am afraid."*

— Audre Lorde

Who hasn't dreamed of traveling the world, or even of working and living abroad? Those daydreams are often painted in warm colors: slow walks on cobblestone streets, the aroma of unfamiliar spices in the air, the coffee sipped from colorful mugs at a small table where no one knows your name. We romanticize life abroad and turn it into a dream. What rarely finds its way into those daydreams are the invisible moments and challenges that women living and working abroad encounter every day.

In this book, you will read the stories of women from different countries, diverse backgrounds, social

1

statuses, and professional aspirations. You will notice one common pattern across all of those individual situations – one that is part of a larger problem – documented in data but rarely discussed openly, especially when it comes to women living and leading abroad.

Across borders, highly capable women face pressure from systems that undervalue international women's leadership. Without support, they are forced to constantly prove themselves, stretch to fit in, and slowly lose confidence and their identity along the way.

Despite decades of progress, worldwide, women remain significantly underrepresented in senior leadership roles at all levels. They receive less career support and fewer opportunities for promotion. According to McKinsey & Company's *Women in the Workplace* report, only 29% of women hold C-Suite positions globally (McKinsey & Company, 2025). Although this figure has improved marginally over the years, it shows a lack of appreciation for the multifaceted leadership skills women bring to the table.

These numbers alone are sobering. But for women living and working abroad, the challenge goes even deeper. Research on expatriates and international leaders is surprisingly limited.

Global professionals remain invisible in terms of their challenges and are getting lost in the broader leadership data. When it comes to women, the challenge is amplified.

Women are left alone and forced to deal with gender biases that limit their access to power, face cultural biases, and deal with structural barriers with unspoken expectations.

A woman may be highly experienced, multilingual, culturally intelligent, and resilient – yet still be told she is "not ready," "too different," or "not visible enough." She may watch less experienced colleagues advance faster, not because they are better leaders, but because they fit the unspoken leadership prototype in that environment.

The Impact on Women

Having worked with international women for two decades, I've seen how much this problem affects the lives of women professionals and how deeply it impacts their personal lives. The negative mantra of being undervalued, underpaid, and underestimated follows the women abroad. They don't see a way forward, doing the same things over and over again to prove themselves, without success. The constant feeling of being "a stranger", the loneliness, and the lack of recognition for their efforts and expertise are ever-present. Then they come home feeling angry, frustrated, venting, and willing to quit. This combination leaves women feeling depleted and unfulfilled, wondering whether they made the right choice in working abroad. Both their personal and professional relationships suffer, leading to a cycle of despair.

They lose hope, and as data shows in global trends, they withdraw from their aspirations and stop fighting.

Here is a story that was shared with me and

remained with those who witnessed it. Use your imagination and try to feel what women felt there. This occurred in an international company, in a multicultural environment, with women from different countries and backgrounds all in the same office. A senior leader and a young woman were discussing work when he suddenly pulled her onto his lap in front of the entire team. She was silent, confused, and frozen.

The silence that followed was deafening. There was confusion, fear, and anger on her colleagues' faces. Everyone felt it – the violation, the imbalance of power, the impossibility of the situation – but that man in a leadership role seemed oblivious. The room was heavy with unspoken tension, discomfort, and disbelief.

That woman's response to the situation was shaped by her culture of respect, harmony, and compliance. When this inappropriate behavior occurred, her immediate instinct was not to confront but to endure. For her, silence was the most responsible choice at that moment. Was it weakness or was it survival that she learned at the intersection of cultural expectations and power dynamics?

What went unseen was the cost of carrying that discomfort alone. By staying quiet, she ended up carrying the burden that really belonged to the system.

This story is not about modesty or cultural norms. It is about how capable women, especially those working across cultures, are often left to navigate abuse without protection. They are expected to adapt, absorb, and move on. Notably, the incident was never addressed afterward.

That moment wasn't just inappropriate — it was a reminder of the vulnerabilities women face in professional spaces, even in international and multicultural environments. It shows how power can be misused, boundaries ignored, and confidence shaken, and why creating frameworks that protect, empower, and guide women in leadership is so essential.

An international woman living abroad needs equal opportunities, respect, and recognition. It takes more effort for an expat to advance in her career abroad, to establish life, and navigate the cultural challenges. Yet, those efforts go unseen and rarely appreciated.

In today's global world, respecting and acknowledging different opinions, cultures, and unique perspectives is not optional. We have to embrace the richness that it provides to the organization and normalize acceptance in our workplaces.

The Impact on Companies

The impact this has on companies is significant. The data shows that when organizations undervalue, underpay, or underestimate women — especially those with international backgrounds — the consequences go beyond individual careers. Inclusive and diverse teams perform better. The intercultural synergy drives innovation and creativity. McKinsey & Company's research shows that diverse leadership teams are more likely to achieve stronger financial performance, with gender-diverse executive teams associated with a 25% higher likelihood of outperforming industry peers. Academic studies further demonstrate that diverse teams make higher-quality decisions faster than homogeneous teams.

Inclusion matters even more when it comes to the experience of international women in a workplace. They often report feeling unseen and unsupported, which hinders their potential. Simply having a diverse workforce is not enough. Women want to feel valued, heard, and psychologically safe.

If this problem is not addressed, and international women continue to feel undervalued, unsupported, and underrepresented, businesses and societies will stagnate. Underperforming teams will fail to adapt, innovation will slow, high-potential talent will leave, and global opportunities will be missed. Dissatisfied employees and a negative corporate culture hinder businesses' growth and reputation.

In all my years of international experience, I have noticed an obvious lack of professional support for women navigating their careers abroad. There were plenty of training opportunities in general leadership and other professional skills, but none of them were relevant to women's needs or to what they face daily when reporting directly to men abroad.

International women are praised for their resilience, adaptability, and strength. Yet, too many women living and working abroad carry an invisible weight — and the systems around them rarely acknowledge it.

That resilience often turns into over-responsibility. That flexibility into losing yourself. That strength into silence and self-neglect.

Too often, confidence fades — because their work goes unseen, cultural bias is ignored, and they are expected to adapt endlessly while others move forward with ease.

International women have a rare global perspective. They have embraced new environments, learned new cultures, and some have even mastered multiple languages to succeed.

Living abroad gives them an edge they can't always see from the inside.

They rebuild themselves in unfamiliar places, again and again.

They stop defining themselves by where they're from and start defining themselves by how they adapt, connect, and grow.

Women living abroad are resilient and adaptive. Not everyone has that.

If you are a woman living and working abroad, you do.

Now pause for a moment and reflect on your own journey. Answer the questions below to acknowledge your actual experience.

How many times have you hesitated to apply for a higher position?

____

____

____

____

How many times have you silenced yourself because of your accent?

____

____

____

____

How many times have you felt like you were not good enough?

____

____

____

____

How many times has a simple "Where are you from?" made you feel smaller at that very moment?

____

____

____

____

Now that you have answered those questions and have reflected on your own experience, try to imagine the opposite of what has been happening to you abroad. How would a completely different outcome impact you and your family? What could be different?

The Silent Struggles

There are endless stories that illustrate the silent struggles international women face: being undervalued, unseen, and underestimated. Because of bias and cultural expectations, women abroad feel incompetent or simply not good enough.

Kasia, one of my clients, moved abroad with her husband and two boys. She was in her 40s, full of energy, and desperate for a change. As a mother, she took the responsibility of providing for her family to heart and immediately accepted the first job she could get. She put her kids in school, rented an apartment, and took a full-time position at a significantly lower salary than she was worth. Was she happy? Not at all. But she accepted the sacrifice for the sake of her bigger vision. She adapted and neglected her ego for the better future of her family. She supported her husband, who could never find a job that would suit him. Why am I telling you this? Because women like Kasia are real heroes. They prove that even when life is a struggle, they progress in the face of the myriad of challenges. They don't accept " no " as an answer. They never settle for a system's limits and keep pushing their own boundaries for the benefit of themselves and their families.

Kasia got a promotion at her low-paying job, then spent a lot of time preparing for a better career and landed a high-paying job. She did it in an epic manner. She showed up one day at work, and she quit. She felt proud, and she made everyone else feel proud of her because she made it.

Another client, Camilla, was a born leader with strong organizational skills. She landed a job abroad, in an office full of male leaders. Most of her colleagues were men. All of the top leaders were men. They made awkward jokes about young women, spread gossip, and never hesitated to put Camilla in difficult situations. Many times, she shared, she would turn red and wish she could simply disappear. That is how awkward and embarrassed she felt. She could never break through that ceiling of male management. She would never get a promotion. They would never see her grow. Never.

It took her years to quit that job. By then, she was struggling with her self-esteem. She needed help reestablishing her identity — remembering who she was and what her strengths were. And she has gone through that personal transformation. The day she felt confident and proud of herself, her life changed.

The plight of international women living and working abroad affects them and those around them. The effect of this unaddressed gap goes far beyond individuals. Team performance declines, businesses' bottom lines drop, and relationships and families suffer. If we do not change these disparities, the genius that these women can and do bring to their roles and to the global professional community will never be realized.

Chapter 2

From Silence to Strength

"It took me a long time to develop a voice, and now that I have it, I am not going to be silent."

— Madeleine Albright

I have gone through all the challenges of living and working abroad.

Like many international women, I had to constantly adapt to new cultures, new expectations, and new professional rules. I have worked in 6 different countries, across borders, cultures, and industries. Funny enough, all of my managers were men. I have never reported to a woman. This fact alone confirms the global trends and the research data we discussed in Chapter 1. I learned to stretch and to adapt quickly. I never wanted to be like my male managers, but I wanted to have the power they held, which shaped my leadership style as I advanced in my career. I have worked as a sales representative, business developer, revenue specialist, business consultant, manager, business owner, senior manager, department head, executive, CEO, and founder of my own companies. Through various experiences and cultural shocks, I learned that some male leaders felt entitled and so powerful that they considered any behavior justified. I also noticed that men in leadership positions found it harder to break the rules with local professionals, but they felt more at ease with international women. I have no data to support this observation today, but it was my personal experience. I witnessed abuse, harassment, or inappropriate professional behavior in almost every international company I worked for. The hardest lessons I learned came from a lack of confidence and the fear of losing a job. When you doubt yourself and struggle to find your strengths, your voice gets lost. Because you are unsure of your value, you are afraid of losing your job. You think that no other company would ever hire you. You think that you are just lucky. They hired you not because you are skilled and talented, but because they were kind enough to give you a chance. You take it as if no other opportunities exist. You want to prove yourself, to work hard just to show them: "You were right to hire me. I am good enough. I am worth it." But then, taking it too far to the point where they take you for granted, they mistreat you, and your identity doesn't exist outside of this job. You feel sorry for having kids or family, and you apologize for the inconvenience when you get sick or when you suffer from painful periods. You try to work during weekends to finalize something by Monday and impress them. You wish you were available for your bosses 24/7, just for them to recognize your good work. The truth is — this will never happen.

Female leadership would look and feel different when we realize we have the power to bring about real change.

Building my resilience and skills was the only option. The system took over, and I adapted to it. I felt that asking for equality was not yet possible. I kept accepting whatever came my way: more work, more responsibilities, less paycheck, more overtime.

In one of the companies I worked for, I never got the official title of the C-Suite while doing that job for over 2 years. My profile of an international woman did not fully align with how the role was traditionally perceived…This was openly acknowledged and not treated as a secret. The emotional cost of this situation was significant. Over time, the pressure to prove myself and to wait for validation began to conflict with my integrity and values. What appeared externally as perseverance masked an internal struggle shaped by prolonged imbalance, unfulfilled promises, and structural inequity.

On the outside, it looked like success. On the inside, I sometimes felt invisible. I overdelivered and overperformed, while being underpaid and underestimated. I worked for the minimum salary and kept taking on new responsibilities. I accepted flexibility and overtime, and I neglected the benefits I could have as a mother of two. No one cared to support me, no one cared to explain to me what I could have as someone who worked and paid taxes in this country. I was blind, naive, and hardworking. I swallowed my tears, and I jumped out of my skin to prove myself. I ignored my personal life problems and always walked in with a happy smile. I felt like I was not allowed to show a single sign of pain or weakness. I feared sharing my struggles. I looked perfect to my employer: a robot ready to work 24/7 in order to generate more money for the business. This was me.

My growth began the moment I asked:

"Who do I choose to be in this environment?" instead of *"How do I fit in?"*

Growth happened through small, intentional steps:

- Acknowledging my international experience as leadership capital
- Naming my strengths instead of minimizing them
- Redefining success beyond cultural expectations
- Taking visible, aligned actions
- Reflecting regularly without self-judgment

This led to grounded confidence, not forced confidence, which later became the foundation for guiding international women abroad.

It was not enough for me to rely on my confidence and experience. I took concrete actions in order to drive positive change and serve the global leadership community in the most effective way. I earned a Master of Science in Management from the Solvay Business School (Free University of Brussels). I have developed my coaching experience and education and earned the credentials of Professional Certified Coach (PCC) from the International Coaching Federation (ICF) and Certified Executive Coach (CEC) from The Center of Executive Coaching in the United States.

Confidence follows actions. The more I invested in myself, the more grounded my confidence became.

According to the Grant Thornton *Women in Business 2024* report — a global survey of 28 countries — women hold just 33.5 % of senior leadership positions in mid-market companies worldwide. The report also highlights a decline in companies with female CEOs, from 28 % to 19 % in 2024, underscoring how progress at the very top still remains fragile.

If we are not focusing on this problem right now, women's parity in senior management won't be reached until 2053 at the current rate of growth.

To drive this change, it doesn't really matter who you are and what your personal situation looks like. You might be a woman with an international background or working in a multicultural environment. You might be looking to advance your career but doubting yourself. You might be a mother balancing work and life, or a single woman stepping into your first professional ambition abroad.

Across industries and cultures, I have observed the same transformation: women who felt invisible start speaking with clarity, stop carrying the constant pressure or guilt, and step into leadership without abandoning who they really are.

If you're ready to break the cycle, step confidently into your strengths, and lead with impact abroad, this book will guide you every step of the way.

Chapter 3

The ABROAD Methodology

*"If they don't give you a seat at the table,
bring a folding chair."*

— Shirley Chisholm

After years of leading, mentoring, and coaching international female leaders, I created the A.B.R.O.A.D.™ framework — a practical, actionable, and empowering method to help women recognize their edge, reclaim their confidence, and lead globally without shrinking.

This framework is designed to guide women step by step, focusing on identity, visibility, and aligned action. It is not about fixing women, but about helping them see themselves clearly and lead intentionally.

I didn't create the A.B.R.O.A.D.™ framework from theory. I created it by living and working as a woman abroad — and then helping women navigate the same challenges I had gracefully and thoughtfully overcome.

Again and again, this framework would guide women abroad from the dark place of low self-esteem and living someone else's life to the bright side of confidence and respect.

The framework has six steps:

Step 1 – Acknowledge Your Edge

Shift from "I need to prove myself" to "I bring rare value."

If you have managed to create your life abroad, you are a leader. You need to realize that adaptability, resilience, and cultural intelligence are your superpowers.

This step is about recognizing the value you already bring with your unique identity and perspective.

Step 2 – Believe in Your Value

Confidence grows when you can name your value.

When you have acknowledged your value, your confidence follows. Learn to trust your skills, your experience, and your voice, even when external systems undervalue you.

Step 3 – Redefine Your Future Self

Design the leader and woman you want to be.

Decide how you want others to perceive you, what behaviors you want to demonstrate, and what values you want to live. This step is about identity before action. You can choose who you want to be without neglecting your authentic self.

Step 4 – Own Your Actions

Translate your vision into intentional steps.

Plan and implement visible, aligned actions — your voice, your boundaries, and your leadership presence matter more than perfection. Every small step is an investment in your future. Don't forget, confidence follows actions. You are what you do.

Step 5 – Assess with Compassion

Growth comes through reflection and iteration.

Track your progress weekly, celebrate small wins, and reflect on lessons learned without harsh judgment. Learn from your failures and adapt as you progress.

Step 6 – Deepen Your Impact

Amplify your impact and ensure you have created a sustainable system that works for you.

Expand your influence, maintain your well-being, and continue staying fully aligned with your authentic self.

In the next pages, we will explore each step in depth. I invite you to stay open-minded, reflect on your own journey, and apply these strategies to your growth.

Chapter 4

Acknowledge Your Edge

*"The journey of a thousand miles begins with
a single step."*

— Lao Tzu

Moving abroad is a truly amazing experience and one that fuels growth. When you move abroad, you meet yourself again, this time face to face. Your full life is in your hands. You have never been closer to yourself. You are discovering yourself as never before. Step by step, situation by situation, you are surprising yourself with new nuances, either from your own culture or from how you react to the unfamiliar. This process is gold. Embrace it and let your identity reveal itself. Take all the time you need to explore your inner voice, your new emotions, and how your brain and body react to what's coming your way.

Acknowledge that adaptability, resilience, and cultural intelligence are your superpowers.

By living abroad, you've already proven not only those superpowers, but also curiosity and courage. Your cross-cultural perspective is your greatest leadership asset.

Shift from "I need to prove myself" to "I bring rare value."

Your life abroad has already made you a leader.

This step, acknowledging your edge, is about recognizing the value you already bring, instead of underestimating yourself.

Common Stories Women Working Abroad Tell Themselves

"I don't feel like they see me as a real professional. I only have experience in other countries and not here, and that seems to count for nothing. They see me as a junior, an entry-level professional."

"I feel so small when I apply for a job and in every job interview, they look at me as if I am begging them to give me a chance."

"I feel like they will never promote me. I have been doing all the work, and now they have brought in a local guy, given him a higher salary, and asked me to teach him everything I have been doing! So he is getting the job title and salary, and I am getting a 'Thank you' and 'Please onboard him'. How shall I take it? What am I missing? There is something wrong with me."

"I was just lucky to be hired. They will quickly realize I am not worth this job. I need to work extra hard and put in extra hours to prove myself. No other company will want to hire me."

Acknowledgement is the first step in everything you do in life. Everything.

Samantha truly believed that she would never be hired for a management position abroad. She firmly believed the company would only hire locals. She felt small and underestimated her skills. She had a strong case of imposter syndrome that prevented her from applying for higher roles or asking for a promotion opportunity. I knew right away that the gap was that Samantha wasn't acknowledging the value she brought as an international employee. To change that, I asked her to list everything she has done since she left her home country:

1. Relocation: finding a place to live, convincing the landlord, negotiating and signing an agreement in French (the language she didn't speak at that time).
2. Finding a job and performing it in a foreign language outside of her native country.
3. Adapting to a new way of life abroad: new food, new weather, new healthcare system, new laws, new policies, new culture.
4. Embracing new culture at work: new rules and policies, new expectations, new communication style.
5. Signing up for French language courses after work.

6. Connecting with new people to make new friends and find a community to belong to.
7. Finding new ways to spend holidays away from family and friends.
8. Learning to be comfortable alone.
9. Learning to get uncomfortable when with locals: feeling excluded, feeling embarrassed, feeling guilty. Learning to manage your own reaction.
10. Finding the positives in everything around us and seeing the bigger picture to keep going. Building resilience and adaptability to not lose your own motivation.

We looked at that list and identified key leadership skills she has developed and demonstrated over the time of living and working abroad:

1. Organizational and time management skills.
2. Communication: verbal and non-verbal.
3. Cultural intelligence.
4. Emotional intelligence.
5. Resilience.
6. Adaptability.
7. Strategic thinking.

When she reframed her self-perception, she was astonished. She felt power, she felt an immediate boost of energy and confidence, and was ready to conquer the world.

That was just the beginning for her. She realised her

strengths and potential, and acknowledged her unique identity, competitive advantage, and edge.

You've just read Samantha's story. I invite you to take a moment and think about it. How many of her achievements might have felt "ordinary" to her (and to you) at the time? But when we paused and reflected on it, they revealed real leadership in action.

Now, think about your own journey. Your experience may not look exactly like Samantha's — and it doesn't have to. But the principles remain the same: every challenge you've navigated, every adaptation you've made, every uncomfortable moment you've faced has shaped your leadership skills.

Reflect on Your Achievements

In order to create your personalized list, ask yourself the following questions and jot down your thoughts in the space provided:

What have I accomplished since moving or working abroad, even if it felt small at the time?

____

____

____

____

What challenges have I faced that required me to adapt, find an immediate solution, or stay resilient?

In what moments did I show courage, persistence, or creativity?

Write down your responses. Use Samantha's example for inspiration. No need to judge it. Just notice it.

Connect Achievements to Leadership Skills

Now you have your own list of achievements! Look at your list and ask:

Which skills did I rely on to navigate these experiences?

____

____

____

____

How did I communicate, adapt, or manage uncertainty?

____

____

____

____

What abilities am I now demonstrating that would make me a strong leader?

____

____

____

Here are some common characteristics I've seen in my clients. Circle or note the ones that resonate with you — and add your own.

- **Resilience**

- **Adaptability**

- **Cultural intelligence**

- **Communication**

- **Strategic thinking**

- **Emotional intelligence**

- **Organization**

- **Time management**

- **Project management**

- **Financial literacy**

- **Problem-solving**

- **Risk management**

- **Other:**

It may be difficult to accept and appreciate your own accomplishments and talents. It depends on your unique culture, personality, habits, and the environment you are in. This is why I would like to take some time to reflect on gratitude and appreciation.

This small reflection will shift your mindset to support your transformation and growth, which is already happening within you.

Gratitude and Appreciation

Gratitude is a positive emotion, a feeling of thankfulness, often for something or someone that has positively impacted your life. It is often confused with appreciation, which is a more general sense of recognizing the value or goodness of something or someone. Gratitude can be seen as the underlying foundation for appreciation. As you explore this step, I would like you to reflect on the concept of gratitude and what it means to you.

How many times have you expressed gratitude or appreciation today?

____

____

____

____

What about over the last few days, weeks?

We often forget what appreciation is. Not because it has no value, but because we are not wired to regularly recognise this feeling. We aim for more, we want to achieve more, to jump higher and run faster. All this suddenly changes the moment something goes wrong. The moment we lose what we once had without considering its value and how grateful we are to have it, we immediately regret not appreciating it enough.

Let's use pure drinkable water as an illustration of this concept. We take it for granted. We know we can get it at any time, anywhere, unless we face a situation where it is not the case. It is, of course, hard to enjoy drinkable water every day when you get used to having it as a commodity. But what if we shift our mindset? What if we slow down, turn off the noise around us, and consciously choose to notice and appreciate what we already have — while it is still here?

Appreciation and gratitude tell us about who we are and bring us closer to our purpose.

Every single day, we have a chance to express gratitude. For things that shape us and make us better people, for things that help us keep up with life, for those who support us and love us no matter what. Gratitude humanizes us, makes our efforts visible, and gives us hope.

Appreciation helps us find hope.

Let's pause and take some time to show gratitude and appreciation.

What are some material objects you are grateful for in your daily life?

____

____

____

____

Who would you like to say *thank you* to today?

____

____

____

____

What things make your life meaningful?

What would you like to be appreciated for?

Taking the time to reflect on gratitude and appreciation allows you to see your journey in a new light. By acknowledging what you've learned about yourself, the challenges you've faced, and the talents and skills that have brought you to where you are, you shift your mindset from self-doubt to self-recognition. This is not just a feel-good exercise — it is a foundation for confidence, clarity, and intentional leadership.

My Appreciation Board – Life & Career Abroad

REFLECTION AREA: WHAT I'VE LEARNED ABOUT MYSELF ABROAD

Guiding Questions:

- What surprised me about myself?
- How did I change emotionally or mentally?
- What patterns became clear?

Key Moments / Examples	What This Says About Me	Appreciation / Gratitude

REFLECTION AREA: CHALLENGES I'VE OVERCOME

Guiding Questions:

- What felt impossible at first?
- What tested my confidence?
- What did I survive?

Key Moments / Examples	What This Says About Me	Appreciation / Gratitude

REFLECTION AREA: STRENGTHS & SKILLS THAT CARRIED ME

Guiding Questions:

- What skills did I develop out of necessity?
- What strengths kept showing up?

Key Moments / Examples	What This Says About Me	Appreciation / Gratitude

REFLECTION AREA: WHAT I APPRECIATE ABOUT MYSELF

Guiding Questions:

- How did I treat myself during hard times?
- What inner qualities stayed consistent?

Key Moments / Examples	What This Says About Me	Appreciation / Gratitude

REFLECTION AREA: EXPERIENCES THAT SHAPED ME

Guiding Questions:

- What expanded my worldview?
- What lessons couldn't be learned at home?

Key Moments / Examples	What This Says About Me	Appreciation / Gratitude

As you create your own appreciation board, remember: this is your story, and your growth is already happening. Pay attention to your inner voice and embrace the nuances of your reactions, your emotions, and your discoveries. Let this reflection guide you to see yourself as a capable, resilient, and evolving leader. You are closer to your authentic self than ever before, and every insight, every appreciation, and every acknowledgment is a step forward in claiming the confidence and leadership you deserve.

Challenge for Step 1

Take a quiet moment and reflect on what you have learned about yourself. Say it out loud:

Adaptability, resilience, and cultural intelligence — are my leadership superpowers.

It's so easy to lose yourself when you are abroad. You may feel intimidated by the new culture and the locals who have it all. You are finding yourself in a constant process of overthinking and adapting, as the way we think, communicate, and make decisions is deeply rooted in our culture. Your brain works non-stop, and you are simply exhausted.

Many of your efforts go unseen and unappreciated. Acknowledging your strengths, your unique qualities, and the efforts you have put into building your life abroad is a crucial step to finding yourself and reconnecting with who you are. Your international background and experience, your courage to live and work abroad, are your biggest differentiators.

By acknowledging your leadership edge, you are claiming your value and opening up your hidden capabilities — your great potential.

This is the first step to your successful future. No matter where you are at the moment, you are stepping into a fulfilling life that you truly deserve.

Chapter 5

Believe In Your Value

"You are not here to shrink down to less but to blossom into more."

— Oprah Winfrey

Many women struggle to see and believe in their own value. We are not taught this way. Often, we are raised with ideas of modesty — of wisdom, if you like. Even as I write this book in 2026, society expects a woman to be silent, compliant, and accommodating. Success and strength look different for women. We are taught not to take up too much space and to make sure we are not too confident — because confidence, we're often told, doesn't look good on a woman.

First, we are good girls. Then we are good wives and mothers. We are expected to be role models of good behavior. The standards society places on us are incredibly high.

And we also have to look good. The cosmetics

industry is booming, adding yet another layer of pressure — how our lips, cheeks, and eyebrows should look. Nails and hair — you can't ignore them. You have to be on top of everything. Add high heels and tight skirts to the mix, and there you go — exhausted but ready to build your career.

When you are not in control, you may start to feel like you are never good enough — constantly chasing trends and putting your energy into becoming what society tells you you should be.

Over time, this creates a quiet pattern of self-doubt. Your achievements are minimized, and your real strengths are ignored. Instead of saying *"I earned this,"* many women say *"I was lucky,"* or *"I'm not ready yet."* Believing in one's value can begin to feel uncomfortable, even undeserved.

For women living and working abroad, this challenge is often amplified. New cultures, unfamiliar rules, language barriers, and unspoken expectations can slowly erode their confidence. Being "the foreigner" adds another layer of visibility and vulnerability. When feedback is unclear, support is limited, or opportunities feel out of reach, it becomes easy to internalize the message that you are not enough — even when you are more than capable. You may feel lost in the crowd. You may get confused about what is expected from you due to cultural misunderstandings and misalignments. Lack of confidence often prevents women from asking the right questions to clarify what is important.

Once you acknowledge your strengths, this step is easier than you think. Your confidence comes from realising your greater potential. You are no longer feeling small; you are seeing your unique intercultural identity as a leadership advantage.

Over the years, working with international women, I have heard their self-doubt. They are different women with different stories — yet they all sound the same:

"I don't even know what I want to do and where I can grow. I have no talents. I used to work hard and do a lot of things at the same time, but I don't think I am talented. I would like to develop myself, but I am simply lost."

"When they asked, "Why do we need to hire you?" I had nothing to say. I felt like "Indeed, why?" I felt awful and turned all pink. I could barely say a word and completely stumbled upon that question. I admire how my colleagues behave - they seem to be so confident, so reassured with their own value. I don't think I could ever do it like them. Everything just comes naturally to them without any visible effort."

"I was very successful back in my country. But here I don't have any experience. I don't know if I will ever find a leadership role in this new environment. I feel like a beginner."

"They only see me as the wife of a local man. I feel like his shadow. No matter what, they only talk to him and never to me directly. This gives me the impression that I don't mean anything in this society. Will I ever earn their respect as a professional?"

Name Your Value

The doubts international women voice are the result of current systems that were never designed for women to succeed. We live in a world built and designed by men for men. We have been present in the workforce for a bit more than 100 years. The transformation of the systems has been way too slow. We are here now, but the system is not here yet. Unfortunately, we are not taught this. Have you ever taken a course on gender bias and women in the workplace at school or university? I don't recall ever seeing one offered. What are the structural changes that have been put in place to support women in the workplace? Apart from the % Key Performance Indicators,, where HR is chasing managers to select female candidates to look good in the annual report. It looks and sounds ridiculous. Without a structural change and a clear system designed for women at work, none of those KPIs will work, and the parity will not happen until a very distant time in the future, if ever.

For women working abroad, questioning the system is not an option. When you are constantly adapting — to a new country, a new language, a new workplace culture — you are told, directly or indirectly, to adjust, to fit in, to be flexible. So instead of asking *"Is this environment supporting me?"* many women instead ask *"What is wrong with me?"*

I have seen businesses fail to create a structure that accommodates women and ensures equity. I say equity here because we do not need exactly the same system that men have created for themselves. This system, the system created for men by men, has failed us as women, and we all know it. We need equity — different resources, different schedules, different policies and rules to succeed and thrive in our careers.

Most leadership systems were designed by men and for men, and they often fail women. What we see today is not a lack of female leadership, but a lack of systems that truly support it. We need new models.

A common example is when a woman reports to a male leader who still defines success, behavior, and authority through a traditional lens. In these situations, a female leader is rarely able to lead to her full potential, because she wants to outperform her male peers. She is accepting the leadership playbook designed by men for men. She follows the rules and the existing prototype of a male leader. She is not ready to rebel and claim her natural female leadership style, simply because there is no support and no system for such a change. Instead, she learns to adjust, to comply, and to shrink parts of herself to fit expectations that were never designed for her leadership.

There is still no clear, structured way to address this dynamic. The impact doesn't stop at the individual level. Her team may benefit from parts of her leadership — empathy, collaboration, emotional intelligence — yet they will also feel the pressure of the system above her. Leadership cascades. When a leader is constrained, that constraint flows down through the team.

I worked with an incredibly talented woman, Kim, who was working outside her country as a Financial Manager at a bank in Singapore and spoke 4 languages.

Yet, she doubted her value. She reported to a woman who then reported to a man with a very traditional view of how leadership should be executed. That's exactly an example of what I was describing earlier. Kim's manager was constantly under stress and pressure. Her deadlines were sharp, and the work needed to be done and reported up no matter the time of day or the weekend. Based on what she described, it was obvious that her manager adapted her style to fit in and behaved more like a man to comply with the system in which she worked.

What happened to Kim was the result of that cascading leadership system. She was looking for a solution internally. She wanted to improve and develop herself to address the burnout she was facing at work, but this work cannot happen in a vacuum.

She would describe herself as an achiever and top performer. She would often work longer hours and be available for her manager during holidays or weekends. She never got a single word of appreciation for her work. She was constantly stretching and overdelivering, but the demands and expectations followed and grew exponentially.

Over a period of time, Kim tried to implement small adjustments and delegate some of her tasks to the team to see if that could help her breathe. She got coached on delegation skills, on empowering people, and on having difficult conversations. Those were quick fixes that would not solve the underlying problem of self-doubt.

I asked Kim to create a list of everything she does well. If she was not sure, she could seek help from her friends, colleagues, and family. She noticed that everyone would praise her for the same or similar things she did well: the high quality of everything she completed and her attention to detail, her commitment to deadlines — everyone knew they could count on her, and she would do everything she could to get things done.

She then realized that it resonated very well with her personal values and expectations. She was glad she could stay true to herself while still delivering value to others. Her identity was her real value, not only to herself, but to others as well.

The day she realized that — she could name it with confidence.

The next step she took was not to go back and try to change the system or her direct manager. She applied for a different position where her value would be appreciated. She quit her manager and started working with a manager of her choice. Her confidence and fulfillment followed. She quickly understood that staying with the wrong person and doing work that doesn't recognize her value will not lead to a different result.

That realization saved her years of happiness and professional fulfillment. This one step — as simple as this may sound — can take years without the right support and guidance.

I am glad you are reading this book. It means you are ready to believe in your value, and the transformation for you has already started.

Now let's look at your own situation.

Your value needs to be concrete. It should be as clear and as specific as possible. Start small and think of every task you do daily. When was the last time you really nailed a task? Focus on what you have been great at.

This is it!

Go on and keep writing down your small and big wins below.

____

____

____

____

What common threads can you see across all your accomplishments?

____

____

____

____

Once you practice this exercise, your unique value will become more tangible. Don't be afraid to discuss it with the people who know you or work with you. Asking your direct manager or your direct reports will give you great insights into what you bring to the table.

You have already heard most of it in your job or professional assignments. Try to remember the feedback you received a few years ago and how it has evolved over time.

I've done it for myself without really thinking about it. It just happened. I heard from my manager: "Wow! You are so well organized! I admire how you always manage to plan and arrange things in your life and at work." And then one day, when I was showing a new system I put in place, I said: "This is already good enough. But well, nothing is perfect." And my manager said: "Yes, YOU are perfect!" Those were two moments of pride where I connected the dots for myself. I have been an achiever all my life, from the school desk to the "perfect wife and mother award". I have always wanted to do my best in every situation. Of course, it came with a cost, and I quickly understood that perfectionism was not a good thing. BUT. And here is the big BUT. If this is who I am, and if it gives me fulfillment and happiness — let it be. "Perfect" may not be the right word in the end. I want to ensure that my actions align with my values. If I do something, I want it done so that I feel I have put my heart and soul into it. I realized that value helped me in many situations in life and work. My managers trusted me because they knew I would go the extra mile. You don't need to ask me twice; I will deliver the best-quality work because that is who I am. I noticed over the years that my value was in making things happen. If something really needs to happen, I would be in the lead. Over time, I developed that value into something even more meaningful. I would find the right people to work together in a synergistic way to make great things happen. Perfection in creativity and innovation, perfection in getting together, perfection in diversity of people, approaches, and skills. All of that amplified my value and deepened my understanding of who I am and who I choose to be.

The most important step is to name your value. Say it out loud. First, say it to yourself. "I am someone with great organizational skills. I can organize anything, no matter the size and urgency."

When you have done it for yourself, then tell your friend or colleague. Be loud about that, as the more you repeat it, the more it becomes your second nature. You start believing in it with your positive affirmations. When others confirm this to you, it suddenly feels real.

You can have more than one value. The art here is placing them in order. Focus on what is the most obvious or frequent thing that you do well. Don't make your list too long; list from 1 to 5 or 7.

What I know, I do well.

____

____

____

____

What others think I do well.

____

____

____

____

What I want to be known for.

____

____

____

____

Now look at this list and reflect:

Out of all of that, which one would I really love to be associated with in the first place?

____

____

____

____

What is the most attractive to you?

What is your biggest potential for development?

Identify your strengths, values, and transferable skills.

Clarify what *you* uniquely bring to the table as an international professional.

Challenge for Step 2

Take a quiet moment for yourself. Say it out loud and feel it as you speak:

I am great at … because … and this is the value I bring.

What you choose to claim shapes how you lead. When you recognize your strengths, values, and transferable skills, you begin to believe in your value and find your voice as the woman and leader you are becoming abroad.

Chapter 6

Redefine Your Future Self

*"If you are always trying to be normal, you
will never know how amazing you can be."*

— Dr. Maya Angelou

For many women, moving abroad is one of the bravest acts of freedom they will ever take. Initially, it looks like independence, opportunity, and an adventure. And yet, once abroad, a new kind of constraint often appears — invisible rules and cultural expectations that internalize self-doubt and blur identity.

This chapter is about realizing your greater internal freedom: the freedom to define who you are becoming, to step outside predefined roles and cultural norms, to choose yourself — even when the world around you subtly asks you to shrink and to fit in. Redefining your future self is where real freedom begins.

What have you personally done to become free?

Maybe you moved abroad for this reason or left your parents and started living on your own. Or you made some life choices to claim your freedom.

But can you honestly say that you are internally free today? And what does it mean to you?

Think about it.

The biggest discovery I've ever made about my freedom is that I am free to make my own choices.

You are free in your choices.

You always have a choice. You can choose who you want to be or to become. Remember this and write it down in a visible place:

"No one can choose on your behalf. You are always in control of your choices. *You.* No one else."

How does it sound to you?

This realization will help you move forward with this chapter. It is essential to understand the freedom you have today and the choices you will make after reading this book.

We are who we think we are, and we believe ourselves to be who we think we are.

Read this again and try to understand this concept.

Our thoughts shape our beliefs.

Our identity is shaped by what we think and believe about ourselves.

What does it mean to you?

If we think of what is in our power and control, this

is it. We cannot control our genetics, but we can control who we become and how we evolve by changing our thoughts and beliefs.

What a great discovery!

We are in control of who we are if only we can control our thoughts.

When we control our thoughts, we control who we are.

Now, how do we get to control our thoughts? Let's see an example.

This morning, I am stressed because I need to be on time to drop my kids off at school, then get to work, and the day is already packed with commitments. I think I may be late, so I try to put some pressure on my kids to hurry up, but then I get stuck in traffic, and we are late anyway. I think, 'What a terrible morning!' and it sets the tone for my whole day. My kids are upset with me being stressed; everyone is stressed in the end, and the mood goes all the way down. What did I learn from it?

The next day, a similar situation. I wake up earlier and get prepared to work with some positive affirmations:

'What a great day it is going to be. I am looking forward to listening to my favorite music on the way to work. I smile at my kids, and we drive to school singing together. I tell them how happy and excited I feel about today's busy day. They respond with a question in their eyes, and I explain to them how I learn to control my thoughts. We discuss some funny examples of difficult situations and how we could teach our brains to respond differently and leverage a smile each time. We still get stuck in traffic, but as we are enjoying our chat, it all goes unnoticed, and we get to school in a positive mood. The result? We've built our bond while discussing negatives, and this little chat minimized the impact of those on our lives.

Zooming out the situation and generating positive thoughts helps us gain control over our life.

Think of the last time you felt really down, stressed, or frustrated. Using the example above, how could you have reacted differently?

____

____

____

____

What thoughts could help you change your experience overall?

How will you try this approach next time you have a difficult situation?

Write down 5 positive affirmations that you will use in the morning to set up the tone of your day.

What is the cost of not taking control?

I've seen women living the life they never wanted in the first place. I've seen them stretch too much and lose themselves to the daily needs of others.

You don't want to be someone you don't like. You are not going to become happy living a life that does not feel like yours.

I worked with Kristina, who always felt depressed and homesick. She would always come to me to vent. Her complaints were different, but I could clearly catch a common thread. The people around her shaped her identity. Her husband liked her long hair and would ask her never to change her hairstyle. Her mother would always expect her to come home for all holidays; she never bothered to check the ticket prices from London to Riga or the arrangements required to make it happen. Kristina's manager asked her to support him with all late-evening dinners and customer presentations. Of course, that time was not paid. She would often have to take notes and send invites - doing the job of a secretary, even though this was not even close to her responsibilities as a graphic designer. She felt overwhelmed and bound by her responsibilities and commitments. She wanted her mother to be happy with her. She wanted her husband to love her. She wanted her boss to appreciate her for how hard she worked. The problem was - she never felt good about herself. All those actions she took didn't bring her fulfillment, and never added value to her life. Her choices always depended on other people's opinions.

One day, we sat together and made a plan. We went through this step together, and within about a month, we could see her happy face again. There were a few tough moments along the way of her transformation, but that would gradually change.

We are going to change it for you, too. This technique works 100%. There is no magic here. It is all about who you are and who you want to be. Set realistic but aspiring expectations. Dream big and be bold.

Design the Leader and Woman You Want to Be

Before you can act with confidence, before you can step fully into your career or life abroad, you need to know who you are and who you want to become. This is about finding your identity before taking action: deciding how you want others to perceive you, what behaviors you want to demonstrate, and what values you want to embody.

You have acknowledged your edge and believed in your value. This belief becomes the foundation for your voice abroad: the way you speak, the decisions you make, and the presence you carry in meetings.

Imagine yourself as a painter, and your life as a canvas. First, paint your present self — all the elements that make you who you are today: your habits, routines, commitments, relationships, strengths, and passions.

Then, take your brush and add or remove elements to reflect the version of yourself you want to become. Which habits will you strengthen? Which commitments or patterns no longer serve you? What people or hobbies drain your energy and waste your time? What people, aspirations, and hobbies would you like to bring into your life?

There is no right or wrong way to do this. Let your imagination guide you. This is a visual reflection of who you are today and who you are becoming, a step toward designing the leader and woman you want to be.

I invite you to start creating your better version below. Design yourself.

How do you want to look? Go deep into details: hair length and colour, style (classic, casual, modern, other), make-up / no make-up.

____

____

____

____

How do you want to be perceived? Personality: friendly, sociable, trustworthy, reliable, respectful, distant, serious, intelligent, easy-going.

____

____

____

____

How do you want to feel? Important, relaxed, always on the move, busy.

____

____

____

____

What lifestyle do you want to have? Gym and fitness, healthy food, traveling a lot, working hard, staying home and relaxing, reading in my cozy place, close to nature.

____

____

____

____

What type of leader do you want to be? How do you want others to describe you when they speak about your leadership? Trustworthy, serving leader, attentive to people, motivational, inspiring, confident, intelligent, easy to work with, affirmative, visionary, supportive, promoting growth and development, caring for team and individuals, challenging.

____

____

____

____

Write down everything that comes to your mind. Don't think too long. List it all and trust your intuition. Your unconscious voice knows all the answers already.

Now you can become *her*. This is it. Your *role model*, your *better self*, is ready for you to go.

Challenge for Step 3

Close your eyes and imagine your future self.

What will you look like?

____

____

____

____

What will you say to yourself today?

____

____

____

____

How do you feel right now?

____

____

____

____

When we as women redefine our future selves, we are recalibrating our trajectory. We are creating the lives we want to live, the lives we deserve. We start managing life through informed decisions.

Chapter 7

Own Your Actions

*"In the long run, we shape our lives, and we
shape ourselves. The process never ends
until we die. And the choices we make are
ultimately our own responsibility."*

— Eleanor Roosevelt

Many of us go through life without fully owning our actions. We let circumstances, other people, or external expectations dictate our choices — and then we blame ourselves when things don't go as planned.

There is an easy way to find excuses for things that are not happening or not working exactly the way we want them to. Most of the people I worked with would come up with at least one reason not to take action. It is usually "This is not the right moment", "I am too busy with my work", "I first need to learn the language", "I want to first buy a house", "It is because I am not local, it is easier for those who grew up here. I will never get there." "Things are just the way they are. I can't do anything about it."

When we refuse to claim ownership, we give away our power, our confidence, and our ability to influence outcomes. We become passive spectators in our own lives instead of leaders — both professionally and personally.

Owning your actions means translating your vision into intentional steps. It's not enough to dream or wish for something to happen. If you are not doing anything to make it happen, you are not going anywhere.

Now that you have designed your Future Self in Chapter 6, it's time to act on it. Ask yourself this question to guide you in the right direction:

How do I get from where I am today to where I want to be?

____

____

____

____

List everything that comes to your mind. Below are some examples to get your thoughts percolating.

1. Take a course to get that new skill
2. Get a degree in…
3. Learn a language
4. Apply for a position of..
5. Update my LinkedIn profile and my CV
6. Reach out to 10 companies per day
7. Call that person that I met, and ask …
8. Throw away all my clothes and buy what I want, to look like I really want
9. Open a savings account and save x amount of money monthly
10. Subscribe to a gym and go there 2x per week

Record your thoughts in the space provided below.

____

____

____

____

Those actions must be clear, realistic, and concrete. If you list something, think about how it will bring you closer to the better version of yourself. Those actions are not simple tasks.

You are building habits, small actions that you will repeat daily, weekly or monthly and will become part of your routine. They will become your natural habits, and this is your goal. Your habits will shape who you are and will lead you to a better version of yourself. The version you have designed is based on who you are.

Your actions are fully your responsibility. Waiting for things to be perfect is not an option. "I will do it when I have more time." Don't even think about it! You will always be busy. You will never have enough time. I wanted to earn a Master's Degree in Management, but I always felt I was too busy for it. I had too much work, kids to take care of, and language courses to follow. There was one day when I said to myself: "Enough waiting for that perfect moment that will never arrive. I will do it this year". Guess what happened? I made clear agreements, set boundaries, and defined my terms. I made it in one year and proudly hung my diploma on the wall of my office.

I still had kids, I still had my work, I still had my responsibilities. I paused my language courses, I stopped doing home chores, and outsourced them to my husband. I stopped spending time where it was not important. I planned every day and ensured I had enough time for life-essential activities and for healthy sleep. It was a tough year for everyone — we had to adapt and adjust our expectations. But we still managed to enjoy quality holidays together — and everyone agreed it was absolutely worth it. When I saw my daughters and my husband crying with pride at the graduation ceremony, they felt for me, and I felt for them. I did it not only for myself, but also for them. Those achievements, those stretching moments of growth — they make a family stronger, and they bond us. They looked at me the way they never did, and I, in turn, looked at them with great appreciation and gratitude.

Your voice, your boundaries, and your presence matter more than perfection.

Every small action you take is an investment for the future you want to create.

I have noticed the same patterns among women abroad when it comes to finding time and energy for things outside their current jobs and families. Those internal excuses seem to sit so deep in their minds that it is almost impossible to get them into action.

Over the years, those are some of the voices I've heard again and again in my work with women abroad — self-doubting thoughts and limiting beliefs that gradually limit potential and influence decisions:

"I work every day, and by the time I get home, I feel tired. I don't want to be even more tired. So I spend all my free time hanging out with my friends and watching movies. Sometimes I travel too. But that is it. I don't have time for anything else."

"When do people find time to study and work on a side hustle? I barely have time to see my family. I am always busy — from morning to evening, it feels like I am running a marathon. This will never end. I feel exhausted."

"I have to constantly learn and adapt to this new life. I spend all my free time reading and translating invoices, documents, and bank statements. I am getting tired just thinking about it. If I get to read a book or watch a movie, this would be during holidays."

"I am so distracted by my friends and family. We have different time zones, and they keep texting and calling me when it is the only free time I have. Sometimes very late at night. And then Facebook... I spend hours following my friends and posting updates on my life abroad. I can't help myself but constantly check what's up there."

The Paradox of Time

What is your relationship with time? I want to focus on this topic specifically in this step, as I have noticed time being the biggest obstacle and a blocker for my clients. It is hard to manage your life if you do not control your time. If your agenda doesn't belong to you, you are not able to prioritize or make the right choices.

Free time is not given. How much free time do you really have? And when you think about your free time, does it make you feel stressed or excited? For most of us, it is usually both. We worry about not having enough time. And at the same time, we dream of using our free time for the things we truly care about.

The paradox of modern life is that we don't always see where our time actually goes.

A "quick" social media check easily takes one hour a day.

A traffic jam adds another hour or two to an already full agenda.

Cleaning an inbox of 1,000 emails or sorting through years of photos can consume an entire weekend!

Unfortunately for all of us, the 24-hour rule cannot be changed, and sleep is non-negotiable if we want to function well. I personally sleep 7-8 hours per night. It doesn't work all the time, but this is my "normal". What is your normal sleep time?

Time is precious and scarce. So what can we do about it?

Think of time as your budget.

Imagine your free time as money. Every day, you receive a wallet filled with a certain number of free hours. The question is rather simple:

- How will you spend them?
- Can you invest them wisely?
- Can you save some and use them later?
- Can your actions today create more free time tomorrow?

This is what owning your actions looks like in practice.

A small change can lead to a big gain

Let me give you a concrete example.

Every day after work, I used to stop by a grocery store, decide what to eat, and then cook at home. Some days it was really quick. Other days, the store was crowded, I felt tired, and I didn't know what to choose. I would sometimes spend more than an hour there. What should have been a simple task often consumed my entire evening. So I decided to change one small habit.

Every Saturday, I now plan my meals for the next seven days. I write a grocery list, choose simple meals, and make sure dinner takes no more than 30 minutes to prepare. This planning takes me about 30 minutes. I then do all my shopping in one go. The result is amazing. I save five to six hours every week. Those are the hours I now use to read, rest, or do something meaningful.

One intentional action created extra time for me.

Another example is ironing. I used to spend hours on it. I then questioned this practice in its essence. I hate ironing, and I don't see the value of it. I threw away my iron, and I stopped buying clothes that require ironing. It's a system of choices that helps you gain time and invest it in something meaningful.

That is leadership in everyday life.

Now It Is Your Turn: Identify Your Time Wasters

To own your actions, you first need awareness. Ask yourself:

- What activities drain my time without giving me much in return?
- Where do I lose time without noticing?
- What habits keep me busy but not fulfilled?

Now take a pen and paper and put it into action.

List your biggest time wasters.

____

____

____

____

For each one, think of one alternative.

____

____

____

____

Estimate how much time you could save.

Set a realistic goal.

There is one important step left here. Now that you know where you can save time and where you can gain it, replace time-wasters with activities you want to do. Those should be the activities that will get you from where you are today to your Future Self. Look back at Chapter 6 and define the actions and — not just things you think you should do. And you should review your time budget every two or three months.

As your life changes constantly, and your priorities evolve, your time strategy should evolve too.

Flow is your best friend.

Have you ever heard of the concept of *flow*? Flow is the state of being fully immersed in what you are doing. Time disappears. You feel focused, creative, and absolutely happy. Many people think flow just happens. But it doesn't.

Flow is the result of intentional choices.

You can experience flow in your work, learning, or anything you do. You can even experience flow with friends — when connection feels effortless and energizing.

You can create your flow.

Ask yourself:

- Where do I spend my time?
- Who do I spend it with?
- What activities energize me rather than
  drain me?

Now think about your objectives. Are there activities you are not doing today that could move you closer to who you want to become? How do you create a system that allows you to focus on those activities fully?

To get into your flow, you need to plan for it. Establish rituals and triggers that will help you focus. Remove all distractions, switch off your notifications, and put away your phone. When you focus on something for a long period of time, you get to the essence of it. You start to understand it better, master it, and finally get creative. Whatever you do on the way to your transformation — don't look for perfection but rather for a flow state. Try to reach excellence by practicing more, documenting what you learn, and finding better ways to do it.

You cannot control everything in life, and there is no point in trying.

But here is what you can always choose:

- How you spend your time
- What you prioritize
- Where you say yes
- Where you say no

Once your objective is clear, decisions become easier. Every decision you take, every choice you make — think if it serves your Future Self. How will it bring you closer to your vision?

Every choice leads somewhere, right? So simply ask yourself:

- Where does this choice take me?

This is how you own your actions and how your confidence becomes visible.

The moment you realize you can control your choices, your time, your priorities — your transformation has been achieved. This is the golden part and the breaking point of your mindset shift. From this point of control, you realize you can also influence your potential. You can dream bigger, take bolder moves, and decide what is right for you. You are no longer limited by your own beliefs. You are no longer stuck in your own box. You can plan for 1 year, 3 years, 5 years, or a decade. How will you want to look and feel in 10 years' time?

This moment is empowering. You feel freedom and clarity.

What you do shapes who you are. Who you are becoming will shape what you will do next. You now fully own your actions and the outcomes.

Challenge for Step 4

What is one action you have identified that you will do next?

____

____

____

____

How important is this action to you?

____

____

____

____

What will be the cost of not doing that action
right now?

____

____

____

____

What will be the outcome of consistently doing that
action in 1 year?

____

____

____

____

Chapter 8

Assess with Compassion

"Do the best you can until you know better.
Then when you know better, do better."

— Dr. Maya Angelou

As women, we often show compassion to others. It is our natural ability to find warmth, empathy, and understanding for everyone but ourselves. We have been raised in a society with high, if not irrational, standards for women. We have not designed those standards for ourselves. They are grounded deep into the historical past of patriarchy and the male vision of what a woman's life and identity should look and feel like.

This creates a disconnect between our authentic lives and the systems that dictate how our lives should be to accommodate men's needs.

Assessing ourselves with compassion is one way to bridge that gap. If you look at your experiences, choices, and actions with curiosity rather than judgment, you will begin to recognize your courage, resilience, and growth—even when they don't meet external expectations.

Now that you are undergoing a meaningful transformation, it is especially important that you don't lose your direction. You need to gently guide yourself toward your vision and navigate the unknown with confidence and self-compassion. Track your progress weekly, celebrate small wins, and reflect on lessons learned without harsh judgment. Remember that growth comes through iteration, and not pressure. Sometimes we can be too harsh on ourselves. We want things to move fast. We want the results now. We want everything at the same time, and when something goes off track or there is a delay, we blame ourselves, get impatient, and, even worse, become demotivated.

It is a good practice to monitor your progress and celebrate your small steps. If you look at yourself today and compare yourself to the past, what has changed? Usually, it is not difficult to notice how much progress we have made compared to a few months or years ago. This is already a good start. Zoom in and zoom out. Don't forget — this is your competition with your past self. No one else can win it. You are in control, and you define the rules. Be gentle and kind to yourself.

Ana was never happy about her progress. She worked as a Sales Manager managing three teams across the globe. Working remotely was great because she could leverage the flexibility and spend her free time outside of work on valuable activities. She went to the gym 3 times per week. She scheduled online language courses during her lunch break. But she felt as though her efforts were not yielding results. After 6 months of this routine, she still felt like she was the same Ana. She wanted to add more actions and increase the frequency to accelerate her progress. I guided her through the thinking process, and together we identified the root cause of her dissatisfaction. She set high expectations on how fast she would progress, ignoring that everything good and valuable in life takes time. By adding pressure and increasing the frequency of actions, she would lead herself straight into burnout. Instead, she added more reflection moments and quality time with people close to her to celebrate her progress and enjoy her new identity. While before she focused on the outcome, this time she focused on the process and felt proud of the actions she was taking rather than the goal she had set for herself. By changing her routines and integrating new habits, she changed her narrative about who she was. That realization gave her a fulfilling and empowering lifestyle.

Managing your own expectations is something I would like to focus on in this chapter. This will help you to shift your perspective and unlock your potential even more.

"When you have expectations, you are setting yourself up for disappointment!"

— Ryan Reynolds

You are surrounded by other people's expectations for you long before you can realize it. When you are 10-11 months old, everyone is expecting you to start walking. Every day, your parents will make comments about it, while relatives and neighbors will not hesitate to ask whether you have already started walking whenever they see you. Have you ever seen an adult who has still not learned how to walk? How many teenagers are still crawling on the streets, not meeting our expectations to walk at 10-11 months? And what if it is 12 or 14? What difference does it make?

Then it starts with the teeth, grades at school, a first date, marriage, kids, and so on. The expectations of others and our own surround us all, lifelong, don't they?

What would you say if I told you there is only one *big step* to living a happy and fulfilling life? And it is this:

Do not expect anything from anyone. And do not live up to other people's expectations.

Seriously, let it all go. Easy to say, not easy to do. This world is too crowded with overwhelming information, smart people telling us what to do and how to live. Stop giving credit to people who impose their lifestyles and their own vision of success. Open your mind to what is important to you and listen to your inner voice. Embrace the differences between cultures, individuals, and societies. Our expectations are shaped by our environment and the closest people in our lives.

There is a simple way to do a reality check on our expectations. Imagine a life that is filled with disappointment, hate, and violence. Some of us are struggling with it right now. If you have never experienced or seen it, watch a documentary or a movie about how people survive in very hard conditions. Think of the disrespect and evil that people have to deal with on a daily basis. Think of the poorest countries where children struggle to find food or peace. When you envision the dark side of this world and how it makes you feel, you understand that some of our expectations are truly artificial. They don't make us happy; they add pressure and prevent us from enjoying what really matters to us.

Now, when you are on the safe side, let it go. Think of life as a constantly changing flow, not a given environment. Become curious and enjoy the ride.

When you go on holiday, think about how exciting it is to step out of your usual routine and plunge into something new. Do not expect everything to go smoothly, and being happy 24/7 just means you are on holiday and are entitled to it. Create an empty page in your head that will be filled out by every memory you create during that journey. You will feel how rewarding this approach is when you realize you have not experienced a single disappointment, but so many other positive feelings and emotions! What an adventure and a good learning experience for you.

Expectations Are Like a Double-Edged Sword

Expectations can kill or save your relationships. When you are getting married, you have no idea what you are doing and what it will all look like in reality. Your expectations have already been sitting on the bench and waiting to exert themselves over your life. Your partner is not present as much as you expect. You feel disappointed because your flat wasn't cleaned when you came back from a business trip. You didn't receive a call to wish you a goodnight when you went to visit your parents. The list can go on and on. Those are your expectations generated by your imagination of what a family life looks like, what a loving partner would do or not do. What if you free yourself from everything you think *should be* and just *let it be*? How would you feel if everything that happened were a surprise and a delightful moment?

When you have zero expectations, everything good happens as a pleasant surprise.

Let's complete this small exercise.

Ask yourself the following questions and reflect in the space provided.

What is the feeling that I am looking for the most during the day?

____

____

____

____

What gives me that feeling?

____

____

____

____

What can I do to make this feeling last longer or to trigger it?

____

____

____

____

How can I positively impact the people around me?

____

____

____

____

What will I do to let go of my expectations and the expectations of others?

____

____

____

____

Now that you have gone through the assessment of your progress and the understanding of your own and other people's expectations, it is time to create some ground rules for how you will assess your progress with compassion.

Challenge for Step 5

How often do you pause to reflect on your progress?

What do you define as success?

How will you celebrate your small wins?

What will guide you to not lose your direction?

____

____

____

____

Let's pause and reflect together now that you've explored the importance of tracking your progress and assessing yourself with compassion. Take a moment to notice how far you've come. You've seen how expectations — your own and those imposed by society — can become a trap, and you've learned how to shift your focus toward your small wins and concrete steps to growth.

By reviewing your progress with empathy, you honor both your efforts and your journey. This practice strengthens your confidence, helps you align with your authentic self, and reminds you that your voice only gets stronger with every step forward you take on your unique path to success.

Every reflection, every acknowledgment, every compassionate assessment moves you closer to the woman and leader you are becoming abroad. Keep observing, keep celebrating, and keep owning your journey — step by step.

Chapter 9

Deepen Your Impact

"Leadership is about making others better as a
result of your presence and making sure
that impact lasts in your absence."

— Indra Nooyi

Many women believe that their growth and ambitions will be seen as selfish. They are afraid to dedicate time and invest in themselves as this may negatively impact their relationships, families, and work. This belief is fundamentally wrong, and it is deeply rooted in the patriarchal systems that continue to shape society. From a young age, women are taught to put others first, to adapt, to shrink, and to meet standards that were never designed with their needs, potential, or aspirations in mind.

The truth is that investing in yourself is not selfish but rather necessary. When you show up as your most capable, fulfilled, and authentic self, you positively impact everything and everyone around you. Stepping into your own development will reinforce your self-respect and the respect of those around you. It is also a crucial step toward the woman and leader you want to become abroad.

Step into sustainable leadership while staying fully aligned with your authentic self.

You are getting close to thriving in your impactful international leadership. To sustain your progress and ensure you are living the life you actually want, you need a system that works for *you*. The key moment in this strategic step is to establish your rules and boundaries. Of course, you will always have to take into account the interests and needs of other people, such as your family, friends, colleagues, and managers. Taking into account does not necessarily have to translate into creating a system that will work for them.

You have to start with your needs, your interests, and your boundaries. You then discuss and agree on how your system will align with others. Here is the key argument: you will not adapt to others' needs and interests. You will discuss how they will respect your boundaries and ensure your system works for you. You take the lead, and you are in control of your life.

You will never make everyone happy, and you cannot expect others to make you happy either. This is important to reflect upon. Take some time.

This understanding will guide you in shaping your system of healthy habits and strategic planning.

I will share what worked for me here. As a mother and wife, I have always had to adapt my schedule to meet my family's needs and demands. I had the pressure of making it right and meeting the expectations of " a perfect wife" and " a perfect mother". On top of that, I wanted to look "highly professional" and would never bring my life to work. Then I learned that this doesn't have to be this way.

I can have a fulfilling life and still be " a good enough wife", "a good enough mother", and "a good enough professional". There is no perfection that is valued or appreciated after your death. Even if it were the case, would you then care? Your present and future experience - this is what counts. You want to enjoy your life and feel confident and respected. Well, this will not happen unintentionally.

What I have done and what I invite you to do here is the following self-assessment:

How much time do I spend on my strategic plan:
personal development, professional development,
hobbies, health, and wellness?

____

____

____

____

How much time do I dedicate to my family?

How much time do I dedicate to my friends?

How much time do I spend solving ad-hoc problems for other people because they didn't take their responsibilities?

How much time and effort do I spend trying to meet other people's expectations when I am not even sure it adds any value to my life?

____

____

____

____

Now, look at the results and reflect on them.

What would you like to change?

____

____

____

____

How will you implement it in your new leadership system?

____

____

____

____

Who do you need to discuss it with to clarify boundaries and expectations?

____

____

____

____

Embrace a Growth Mindset

To support your development, here is another concept I would like you to explore with me.

Have you ever tried peeling potatoes in a different way? Well, maybe potatoes aren't the best example, but what about some of the habits you use daily? Once I bought a new coffee machine, and I still had my old one working. Of course, with the two coffee machines available, I kept making my coffee with the old one, because I was used to it and it went faster. The new one had unusual buttons and functionalities I was not yet mastering. This is an example of how a fixed mindset works.

We often stick to what worked for us in the past and ignore new approaches. Why? Because we like the feeling of mastery. Mastery is what happens when you repeat the same tasks day by day. You become an expert in that specific task, and you get satisfaction and confidence. What happens if one element of that task changes? You may lose control and confidence.

No one likes losing confidence.

But what if something changes, you try a new approach, and you discover it is much more efficient? And what will happen if you learn that your old way was much better? This curiosity nurtures your growth mindset.

If you don't try, you will never learn.

The fear of failure holds us back and promotes stagnation. When we are kids, we don't have that fear. We crawl, we hit our heads 100 times until we learn about all the different surfaces in the world, and we lick sand and stones to taste them. We burn our fingers just to find out that fire is painful and dangerous. This is how we grow into experienced adults. And then what?

Then we become cautious and overly concerned with not looking silly.

Our ego prevents our growth.

Kids have no ego. They have enormous curiosity. That's how they grow every day.

Adults have an enormous ego, and that's how they stop growing.

What can you take away from that?

____

____

____

____

What was the last time you did something new without the fear of looking stupid?

____

____

____

____

How many mistakes have you made in the past month?

____

____

____

____

What will you do if you have a chance to try a new way of doing the things you master today?

____

____

____

____

How many times are you willing to fail before you get it right?

____

____

____

____

Your growth affects you, but it also affects everyone around you. It starts from your family and friends, and it goes far beyond that individual impact. A leader who is growing impacts the entire team and organization. As a leader, you are always on the spot. People watch you. People notice the change. Leaders serve as role models to their teams and their followers. There are good and bad examples out there, and this is exactly our mission in this book. We want to drive positive change in global workplaces to prevent the waste of human potential, especially the potential of diverse international female leaders.

When you develop yourself, invest in your growth, and celebrate your small steps — everyone notices. You show up as your better version at work. You show up as your better version at home. Happy families, happy colleagues, happy societies. The impact is huge.

Challenge for Step 6

Who will benefit from your growth?

____

____

____

____

How will you notice that your development positively impacts your family and friends?

____

____

____

____

How will you show up at work in your Future Self version?

____

____

____

____

What is one visible change that everyone will notice when you are around?

____

____

____

____

Chapter 10

Coming Home to Yourself —
Wherever You Are

"You belong wherever you choose to stand and claim your space."

— Chimamanda Ngozi Adichie

Living and working abroad is demanding, and it asks women to adapt quickly, quietly, and constantly. Life abroad requires extra effort that remains invisible at the workplace. No one cares if you struggle outside of the office. On top of that, if you happen to be a mother, this becomes your disadvantage, sorry to say, because your manager will place demands on you that cause conflict with your responsibilities as a mother outside of the work day. No one will openly say it out loud, but you will carry the burden of silenced pressure and guilt, together with your manager's disappointment. Over time, that pressure can blur authenticity and identity, and make even the most capable women question their worth. There is no support whatsoever; the system is not welcoming you. You are left alone with your challenges and uncertainty, while the expectations are high from the start. It all looks kind of like a race, a silly competition without clear rules. They do exist, but they are definitely not designed by women, which makes it challenging to even see the logic or relevance in them.

Fighting constant burnouts, watching others progress quickly, and questioning yourself — this is the reality for too many women abroad. Broken relationships and families, negatively impacted health. The constant feeling of guilt and pressure. Tons of vitamins and painkillers, melatonin at night, and magnesium in the morning. A coffee break abuse to disconnect for a moment and pretend life is good when the facts say otherwise. Making it once as a short win but then falling apart and pulling yourself together from scratch, again and again.

"This life is killing my identity."

"Am I really living my life?"

"I am chasing someone else's success."

"I am losing myself. I don't recall who I used to be anymore."

"What am I getting in return? More work..."

And then one day you drop it all. You withdraw, you disconnect, you abandon. Everything sounds and smells the same to you. That cheesecake you used to adore leaves you indifferent. Those Netflix movies you used to watch in the evenings trigger no emotion.

You are not calling your friends because you have nothing to share, and listening to their stories is too much of a mental effort. Your brain refuses to take in any effort.

You are not interested. You don't even know anymore what you are interested in or passionate about. You cannot function like this. You put on a mask and suppress your emotions. You feel empty, you are not present. You are off.

You didn't plan for that. No one prepared you to navigate your life and work abroad. It all suddenly fell on your shoulders, and the system took over.

The journey outlined in this book was designed to interrupt that pattern and break through the system—to replace self-doubt with self-trust and confidence in intentional female leadership abroad.

Each step of the A.B.R.O.A.D.™ framework builds your confidence and sharpens your leadership edge. You begin by recognizing the strength you already carry. You acknowledge your diverse experience, your unique culture, and the effort it took to get where you are today. You find peace with your unique identity. You reconnect with your value. Naming your values and aligning them with your authentic self gives you the freedom you need when you are abroad. No matter where you are, you come back home to yourself. You are whole. You are enough. You are worthy. You redefine who you are becoming based on your needs and aspirations. You take ownership through aligned action. You are in control of your life. You reflect and adjust with compassion, celebrating your progress and managing your own expectations. And finally, you expand and deepen your impact — without losing yourself in the process. You contribute to a better, modern society with sustainable professional workplaces. You are shaking the outdated systems and standards by bringing your value and your example to the world.

Together, we can provide international workplaces that foster a sustainable culture, inspire leaders, and contribute to a happier global community.

This framework is not linear or rigid. You may return to certain steps again and again as your life, career, and context evolve. That is not failure but growth in its essence. Your journey within this book is designed to be an adventure, full of self-reflection, celebration, and fulfillment. You are loved, cherished, and appreciated for who you are. Your life is designed to be successful and sustainable.

Your leadership abroad is not a destination — it is a practice. Once you have the right support and guidance, you master it gracefully. You now navigate the unknown with confidence and clarity. You can find your voice again and amplify your impact for sustainable success that will serve you and society in the long run.

Reflecting on some of the great transformations

women have experienced within this framework, I would like to share one that still stands out to me.

Nathalie was changing jobs because her employer did not renew her contract. She had a small son, and she couldn't afford to stay after 5. Her husband would work long hours, and his office was far away, so the solution was obvious. She would need to be the one to pick up their son after work each day. She stopped her work at 5 sharp and rushed to pick up her son from school. She constantly felt pressure from her boss, who simply ignored her having a family life outside work. She had extra tasks on her desk each week, and she felt the manager was trying to show her how much work the company had, so she felt even more guilty and either worked harder or took work home.

In the end, she just lost that job. Her manager fired her. She was lost when I met her. She was looking for a job where she thought, "They would accept me with a child," and "They will need to require exactly the same job responsibilities I was doing in my past job." She feared change and struggled to see other options. She truly believed her skill set was limited to the job she was doing, and she didn't realize she had transferable skills and the ones she had brought with her from her home country and from moving abroad. She was afraid the new employer would call her manager and that she would receive negative feedback and a poor letter of recommendation if asked. Nathalie struggled to step back and see herself as a whole. She was not sure what strengths and competitive advantages she was bringing. She could not clearly see her value, nor could she put herself at the center. She was adapting and fitting into the system. That journey was painful, full of regret and self-doubt. She felt guilty for losing the job and the income for her family, and at the same time for having that same family and for having to pick up her son from school. That double guilt drained her energy. She couldn't find a way out of this constant state of despair. She was losing herself and losing her voice.

We took all the steps of A.B.R.O.A.D. one by one. Some steps went faster, others needed iteration and deeper work. But gradually, her confidence started to build. She discovered an incredible number of skills and accomplishments she had. She clarified and named her value. The boundaries were identified and established at home. She has internal permission and an external agreement with her husband on how she will prioritize and plan her time. She took action and targeted companies while looking for a job, rather than the ones that "could accept her". She set clear expectations during interviews and received not one but two great offers to choose from. She impressed senior leaders with her confidence, presence, and self-awareness. Her career progressed, but most importantly, she took control of her life. She continues to work through the same framework again and again, as life is too great to stick to one version of it. She is now free to choose what's next and is not afraid to iterate and dream. She is the leader she has designed to be, and that shows up in every aspect of her life.

The A.B.R.O.A.D.™ framework reminds you that you do not need to prove your worth by shrinking, over-adapting, or fitting into someone else's idea of leadership. Your global experience, your cultural perspective, your survival skills and resilience, your unique identity, including your accent - they are not obstacles but your competitive advantage, your leadership edge.

Wherever you are in the world, you are allowed to lead fully, confidently, and authentically.

And the most powerful part of this journey is this:

When you step into your leadership abroad, you are not just changing your own story — you are helping rewrite what leadership looks like for the women who will follow.

Chapter 11

Step Into Your Voice

*"I never dreamed about success. I worked
for it."*

— Estée Lauder

Before you close this book, pause. Leadership growth happens when insights turn into intention.

I invite you to experience a 7-day challenge. It is an invitation for a gentle reset for confidence and clarity. You can spend 10–15 minutes a day and see where it leads you.

The 7-Day A.B.R.O.A.D.™ Challenge

You don't need more pressure. You don't need to fix yourself. You just need a little space to reconnect with who you already are.

Day 1 — Acknowledge Your Edge

Today is about noticing, not judging.

Write down three things you've gained by living abroad.

They can be skills, perspectives, resilience, or lessons learned the hard way.

____

____

____

____

✈

POSITIVE AFFIRMATION:

My experience has shaped my leadership — even when I forget it.

Day 2 – Believe in Your Value

Today, you name your value.

Write down one moment when your work mattered.

____

____

____

____

It doesn't have to be big. It just has to be real.

✈

POSITIVE AFFIRMATION:

I bring value — even when I don't realize it.

Day 3 – Redefine Your Future Self

Today is about exploring your imagination.

Write freely. No editing. Finish this sentence:

One year from now, I am someone who…

____

____

____

____

✈

POSITIVE AFFIRMATION:

I am allowed to grow into a new version of myself.

Day 4 – Own One Small Action

Today is about launching one concrete action.

Choose one small action you can take today.

- Speaking up once
- Asking a question
- Saying no
- Updating CV

My small action:

____

____

____

____

✈

POSITIVE AFFIRMATION:

Small steps count and bring immediate results.

Day 5 – Assess with Compassion

Today is about kindness.

Answer honestly:

What felt hard this week?

____

____

____

____

What felt easier than expected?

____

____

____

____

No judgment. Just noticing.

✈

POSITIVE AFFIRMATION:

I can learn without being hard on myself.

Day 6 – Deepen Your Impact

Today is about connection.

Ask yourself:

Who benefits when I show up more confidently?

____

____

____

____

Let the answer be simple.

✈

POSITIVE AFFIRMATION:

My growth matters beyond me.

Day 7 — Decide What to Carry Forward

Today is about choice.

Write down one thing you want to keep practicing.

Just one.

____

____

____

____

That's enough.

✈

POSITIVE AFFIRMATION:

I don't need to do everything — just the next right thing.

You don't have to navigate leadership abroad alone.

If you are ready to step fully into your leadership and unlock your potential, and would like to have personalized guided support, reach out to me on LinkedIn by searching Ina Saltanava, CEC, ICF PCC, or through my website, GlobalLeaderEdge.com

You can also email me at ina@globalleaderedge.com.

The A.B.R.O.A.D.™ framework is your guide.

Now it's your turn to claim your edge, lead with confidence, and thrive abroad.

Acknowledgments

I would like to express my deepest gratitude to my family, whose unwavering support and love have been the foundation of everything I do. To my husband, thank you for believing in me, encouraging me to follow my dreams, and standing beside me through every challenge and triumph.

To my daughters, your curiosity, resilience, and laughter remind me daily of the joy and purpose in this journey. You inspire me to be the best version of myself, both personally and professionally.

I am also grateful to my colleagues, peers, and mentors who have shared their knowledge, challenged me to grow, and encouraged me to push the boundaries of what is possible. Your insights and collaboration have been invaluable in shaping not only my career but also the ideas and lessons in this book.

Finally, to the international women and leaders who have shared their stories and experiences with me, your courage, resilience, and dedication continue to inspire this work. This book is as much yours as it is mine.

References

1. Grant Thornton. (2024). Women in business: The global picture.
2. Martinez, M. & Hill, A. (2020). Diversity and Inclusion in the Workplace. International Journal of Management, 1(1), 1-3.
3. McKinsey & Company. (2020). Diversity wins: How inclusion matters. McKinsey & Company.
4. McKinsey & Company & LeanIn.Org. (2024). Women in the workplace 2024.
5. Rafaqat, S., Rafaqat, S., Rafaqat, S., & Rafaqat, D. (2022). The impact of workforce diversity on organizational performance: A review. Journal of Economics and Behavioral Studies, 14(2), 39-50.

About the Author

Ina Saltanava, CEC, ICF PCC, is the founder of Global Leader Edge and a leadership coach specializing in intercultural and executive development. With over two decades of experience working internationally, she helps professionals navigate the challenges of leading abroad with confidence and clarity. She is a Professional Certified Coach (PCC), a member of the International Coaching Federation (ICF), and holds an Executive Coach Certification (CEC) from the Center for Executive Coaching in the United States. Ina combines her practical experience with coaching tools rooted in emotional intelligence, cultural awareness, and global executive leadership.

Having built a career abroad while raising a family, Ina understands firsthand the challenges women face in foreign workplaces — from cultural bias to balancing professional and personal expectations. Her own journey shaped her belief that leadership is not about perfection, but about resilience, authenticity, and learning to trust your own voice.

Ina is currently based in Brussels, living her best life with her multilingual and multicultural family — her husband and two teenage daughters.

Through Global Leader Edge, Ina supports expatriate and international leaders in recognizing their strengths, embracing their potential, and creating meaningful impact across cultures. She is passionate about helping her clients gain confidence, navigate career transitions, and lead with presence, while remembering that growth is a journey, not a destination.